Lasagne

Wayne Holloway-Smith

Out-Spoken Press
London

Published by Out-Spoken Press,
Unit 39, Containerville
1 Emma Street
London, E2 9FP

A CIP record for this title is available from the British Library.

First edition published 2020
ISBN: 978-1-8380211-2-2

Typeset in: Adobe Caslon

Out-Spoken Press is supported using public funding by the National
Lottery through Arts Council England.

Supported using public funding by

**ARTS COUNCIL
ENGLAND**

Contents

Love minus love

can still be love if you
hold it up to the light
at the exact right angle –
diamonds winking off its
underside same yellow as
the fox dead and mine in
the one breath I denied
myself staring down its
dragged open chest its
stomach a smirk dumped
in a green recycling bin
Clapham Road side I
go too far often since I
saw you whip your fringe
on the dance floor I'm
finding tumours in each
place I put my finger
I'm picking them out
my minestrone soup my
lentil and tomato stew
before I put spoonfuls of
it in my body I'm crying
at the speed of cars
nowadays into every
hopeless piece of myself –
O Sarah what it takes to
stay alive I can't die well
if you're dancing

Lasagne

too-sad my ribs gift-wrapped
in fatfat – god forgive me
man we were so small and
reckoned our bodies wrong
– too-tight not ours to keep
o lordlord – we grew up
smoking and checking our
waistswaists – your damp
palm mine in its place – you
didn't want this lifelife let's
pretend it's happening anyway
– didn't want this meal let's
make believe: lasagne moving
silent peas across a plate chips
and cheese – I forgot myself
how to eateat and you burnt
calories off your forkfork and
me burning calories off my
fingers – and you set a match
to your own arm – flame –
bellowing up my shoulder
now smoke spilling up over
your browbrow – the edges
of my frame are scribbled
out – we're taking up so
little space turning our
earthearth pink-hot dust
praise be – I can't remember
the girth of our name

An ode then to

I don't want you gone tonight
with your scruffy haircut the smell
of traffic and your big fat voice buried
in this average racket we could have eaten
cornflakes in unwashed bowls you suggested
the madness and harmony of birds I hope you know
I don't know how much we loved each other but
there's a peasouper in my chest the size of Blackheath pubs
a skylark in the look you handed me hasn't left since
that very specific Tuesday afternoon people have been
crying inside and out of your room shut its curtains
against the obscenity of your going I've been weighing a song
between my lungs its sincerest laughter with some pain
been asking questions without saying your name
I've been minuting everything that comes
out its open throat an exultation
of beak-tip and tongue
getting all used up
the more I keep
writing it down

i.m. R. L

Yellow Tiled Kitchen

where the body wants to die first
how did we get down here among
the potato peelings – we slipped off
a thing: the world the cat bowl the
bin licking its pork chops – it's so
full on – soup tingling in the pot
broccoli hot intelligent water – o my
friend if you got liver cancer I got
liver cancer – a creeping history
of the blood – sometimes it's
important to step from one room
to another cross-legged room – two
cups of dirty coffee and cussing our
dads – outside the school kids go
shouting down the fat road – they
are whipping their striped ties above
their haircuts they are feeding way
into their exact futures – we had
something good like that once –
remember – and we're already here:
raising each other from the dead –
ironing each other's confidences like
longline shirts – what if we just
stoppedturnedaround like this right
now – see: all the graveyards

through   the   window   becoming
empty – all of our beloved standing
straight up
perfectly
pressed

For Anthony Anaxagorou

The fear will make the meat grow closer don't be scared

can't stop thinking – of all
the things we didn't ask for
– bad ankles the beige
carpets we're given in rented
rooms – brooms knocking
against the floor from below
– the downstairs neighbour
who hates me – and by
downstairs neighbour I
mean my soul – I mean it
moves around shape and
size of a used up cow – it
gets about pointless and
grazing angry – bones and
blood and absolute udders –
where does all that
shuddering lactose go –

Margot I recall we held first
nose to snout – nostrils
syncopating then our
foreheads touching a long
while – *Knock Knock* you
said *who's there* I asked you
were three years old and I
love you – *interrupting cow*

too old to be allowed not to
be meat – when we met her
Rosie   she had been spared
by an animal sanctuary –
first the stun gun then the
knife   the blood singing
from her neck – we all have
a deliverer this I think was
mine Margot I love you –

Rosie was allowed to live –
in this place we found a
miracle – the downstairs
neighbour had a broom it
disappeared – a hateful pair
of hands with nothing to do
– by which I mean my soul
was being reworked

one day the sanctuary took
eleven orphaned calves – the
way the body produces milk
is that birth activates its
shimmering   membranes
Knock Knock –

there have been many
moments in which – *who's
there* – I asked and my life
got better from some small

arrival – Rosie having never
given birth was meat wasting
away – stun gun they said
cleaver blood on the apron –
she couldn't hope for natural
milk

who's there – your nose
the snout of my soul our
foreheads *interrupting cow* –
Rosie *interrupting cow who* it
turned out suddenly bursting
fed all of the foundlings
four times a day until they
were blown full and happy
then there was nothing to
be scared for – skies – three
more grey hairs on my chin
– a lovely pregnant silence –
a lovely pregnant silence into
which you grew and
eventually told me the
punchline – *moo*

Tube Voice Man

and my whole body is
a group of sudden
musicians striking up a
tune of longing – not
all bad you see – with
snow in your hair snow
in my eyes – trumpet-
solo cymbal – my fright
growing thinner its lurid
reflection on the insides
of my eyelids and keep
seeing the sad   wife of
a dead man – cymbal-
crash   mandolin   my
heart – we know she is
making   her   daily
p i l g r i m a g e   t o
Embankment   Station
snow rain and today I
think I know what it's
like fading like he did –
know   the   spilling   of
m i l k   t h e   g o n e
understanding   at   the
dinner   table   flowers
sunk   at   the   balcony
door – strings   eking
out   a   little   more

9

emotion at this point a
voice – to hear him
again [mind the gap
please] the whole world
is analogue look – I
love you I just need a
hook a use for this
body and its band of
music – a destination
for people to arrive at –
how many minor or
major injuries did he
p r e v e n t   i n   t h i s
inclement weather –
three violins a soft tuba
– an accordion sliding
through my body on
i t s   j o u r n e y   o v e r
Hungerford Bridge the
pea-green   sad-happy
song of being alive

When I die

it's not in the way
we salt our throats
it's not in the way we
wear masks on our
voices or sleep back
to back – suspecting
everything death in
the shorn leg of the
table some type of
sickness in the
bread-mix the set of
tooth brushes
coughs and we
throw each one
sticking deep in the
brickwork rub our
hands – these were
the days I exhaled a
quiet little scream
and it rearranged all
the flowers in the
windows or just the
windows when it's
dark outside you
don't believe in God
so you won't know
about the very old
woman in Mexico

risen from the grave
for the ninth time –
she woke up pissed
licked her cracked
lip and told everyone
to fuck off   – she
was forgiven such
was the love colour-
ing that moment
forgive me too for
seeming ungrateful
when I've come
blinking back again
toward the living
room lifted my eyes
toward the upturned
empty glass we used
to trap a hornet in
at the onset of
spring

Other titles by Out-Spoken Press

Mutton Rolls • ARJI MANUELPILLAI

Contains Mild Peril • FRAN LOCK

Epiphaneia • RICHARD GEORGES

Stage Invasion: Poetry & the Spoken Word Renaissance
PETE BEARDER

Nascent • VOL 1: A BAME ANTHOLOGY

Ways of Coping • OLLIE O'NEILL

The Neighbourhood • HANNAH LOWE

The Games • HARRY JOSEPHINE GILES

Songs My Enemy Taught Me • JOELLE TAYLOR

To Sweeten Bitter • RAYMOND ANTROBUS

Dogtooth • FRAN LOCK

How You Might Know Me • Sabrina Mahfouz

Heterogeneous, New & Selected Poems
ANTHONY ANAXAGOROU

Titanic • BRIDGET MINAMORE

Email: press@outspokenldn.com